JUDGES POSTCARDS
A brief history

There is every chance that the postcard you send home from your holiday started life in Sussex. Since 1902 Hastings has been the home of Judges, one of Britain's leading publishers of quality picture postcards.

When Fred Judge arrived in Hastings in 1902 he could have had little idea of the worldwide impact he was to make on the business of postcard publishing. But Fred was a master with a camera and a natural entrepreneur. Fred Judge was born in Yorkshire in 1872. Photography was always his real interest, and it was while visiting Sussex in 1902 that he made the decision to give up engineering for a career as a photographer.

Fred and his brother Thomas purchased an existing business in Hastings and set up as photographers and photographic dealers under the name of Judge's Photo Stores. Although the idea of sending an illustrated card through the post was not new (the first having appeared towards the end of the nineteenth century) Fred made his mark by setting himself extremely high artistic standards. At first he concentrated on local scenes and activities. Having taken his pictures he would go straight back to the darkroom to make them into postcards – often for sale within a few hours; and the quality of his work was such that passers by would gather outside the shop window for a sight of his latest work.

Technically stunning, and using all the latest photographic technology, Fred's pictures won over 100 medals, and one-man exhibitions of his work were held in London, Washington, New York and Tokyo.

Back in Hastings the business was expanding, necessitating moves to bigger and better premises, culminating in the move in 1927 to the purpose-built factory that the company occupies to this day. Although the building has been developed and extended, the Italianate façade remains a famous landmark on the A259 coast road.

Fred Judge died in February 1950 at the age of 78, having built up an internationally respected company. The business was sold to another Judges photographer, who introduced lithographic colour printing. Then in 1984 Judges became a real family concern once again when Bernard and Jan Wolford took over. It became even more of a family business when their son Graeme, now managing director, joined, followed by Trevor, now sales director. The present management can truly be said to be building on the foundations laid by Fred Judge over ninety years ago.

Judges Postcards Ltd, 176 Bexhill Road, St Leonards on Sea,
East Sussex, TN38 8BN
Tel: 01424 420919; Fax: 01424 438538
www.judges.co.uk

KENT

IN OLD PHOTOGRAPHS

DAVE RANDLE

FROM THE JUDGES POSTCARD ARCHIVE COLLECTION

SUTTON PUBLISHING

Sutton Publishing Limited
Phoenix Mill · Thrupp · Stroud
Gloucestershire · GL5 2BU

First published 2003

Copyright © Dave Randle, 2003

British Library Cataloguing in Publication Data
A catalogue record for this book is available from
the British Library.

ISBN 0-7509-3382-8

Typeset in 11/13.5 Sabon.
Typesetting and origination by
Sutton Publishing Limited.
Printed and bound in England by
J.H. Haynes & Co. Ltd, Sparkford.

Introduction

With its network of motorways, its ferry terminals and now its Channel Tunnel Rail Link, it is easy to think of Kent as a place you cross on the way to somewhere else. At any time in the last two and a half thousand years, a sizeable proportion of the people within its borders were passing through. Some were welcome; others less so.

The Belgae from Northern France established trading links before Christ. The Romans came this way, as did the Saxons, and the English Church was established here when it could find no joy in London. Canterbury is still the seat of the Church of England and is still the first English city many foreign visitors see. In the shadow of its epic cathedral, within its towering city walls, students, street entertainers, market stallholders and shoppers rub shoulders as they have always done. The sense of continuity with Chaucer's pilgrims survives in spite of, but also because of, the thriving high street stores.

If there was a 'melting pot' of ideas and cultural influences in early England, Kent was it; its inhabitants the most exposed to, and – if not the most accepting of – the first to come to terms with those influences.

It should be remembered that the Romans had to have two goes at settling here. Cosmopolitan as the Men of Kent might have been, there is a world of difference between trading arrangements and the imposition of foreign rule. Even today you will find more flags of St George in Kent than Union Jacks. It is tempting to see this as symptomatic of some kind of xenophobia. Rather than a challenge to the non-Kentish, though, it is more a case of showing the colours; of saying 'we're still here' – and, probably more than any other people, embodying the essence of Englishness. Saintly archbishops, vintage motorcyclists, train spotters, morris dancers, cricketers and painters – if it didn't invent them, Kent has them all in abundance. Romney Marsh is alive with twitchers, the Weald with ramblers.

If its importance as a grower has diminished from the days when that depended on proximity to the London markets, the county has carved just as important a niche for itself in the present economy, by adapting its long experience with the management of outside labour forces and 'pickers'. Great farm stores at the likes of Paddock Wood and Mereworth are now the clearing stations and packing points for supermarket-bound fruit and veg, much of it sourced from abroad.

When its own fruit is ripe, pickers no longer descend on Kent from South London. Instead they have to be imported from middle Europe – a bizarre necessity in parallel with those who are importing themselves from the same quarter in search of work. But this kind of dichotomy is just as much part of life in the county. Cross-Channel travel is now so easy and so commonplace that a large proportion of the local customers of England's oldest brewery in Faversham buy its exported products in France, where the lower duty more than covers the cost of the trip.

Duty of any sort goes against the grain in Kent. Smuggling was a way of life in most towns with connections to the sea. The Hawkhurst Gang was six hundred strong and the smugglers in Lydd used to have a public parade of their booty in the High Street. Secret passages link houses, businesses, inns and, especially, churches. Everyone was in on the act. Nowadays the 'excise men' have regained the upper hand – for the moment, anyway.

Kent's been fending off invasions and clearing up after battles for as long as anyone can remember. The county was peppered with V2 bombs in the Second World War and the Battle of Britain was fought above Folkestone and the White Cliffs of Dover. To people all over Britain, these cliffs are the very symbol of Britain and all it stands for.

That war changed things forever. Where once there were two administrative seats – Canterbury for the 'Kentish Men' of the east and Maidstone for the 'Men of Kent' to the west – all secular power now devolved on Maidstone. In the early 1960s both that town and Dover expanded dramatically, with much new building. The number of people passing through had gone from a steady flow to biblical proportions. Dover began to capitalise on this movement of bodies and freight, and wealth started to trickle back into the county's economy.

In the 1990s the perennial plan for a land link with France finally came to fruition with the building of the Channel Tunnel. Dover held its breath, fearing an end to its supremacy. But all that happened was that more people and more freight arrived to take advantage of the new link.

Now Ashford is centre stage. Fittingly for an old railway town, the new cross-Channel rail link has not only revitalised its fortunes but lifted them to unexpected heights. Its convenient geographical location and the delay in continuing the fast link to London have made it the base of choice for European businesses looking to set up this side of the water. Its star is very much in the ascendancy in the new century and it seems destined to become our pre-eminent European centre.

If it is the Garden of England, Kent is also the Gateway; to people, to produce, to ideas and to the wealth of the nation, temporal and spiritual.

This first selection from the Judges Postcards archive reveals the multi-faceted nature of the county – from grand cathedral cities to bucket and spade resorts, Tudor mansion to caravans, steam railways to bustling seaports. The images cover most of the twentieth century, so will prove nostalgic to many, revelatory to others – especially those who have passed Kent by without a glance. Above all, they provide a snapshot of a great county and remind us that much of old England still remains for the new English to explore, to understand and to enjoy.

KENT

IN OLD PHOTOGRAPHS

Despite its close proximity to the M20 motorway, Allington Lock remains an idyllic spot. The Malta Inn has stood on the bank of the Medway since the fourteenth century. Pleasure boats run between here and Maidstone.

Even on a day like this one you'd be hard pressed to find this much parking space in Appledore nowadays. This is the Black Lion in 1970.

Opposite: St Peter and St Paul at Appledore stands on the site of a Saxon church mentioned in Domesday, though no trace of the earlier structure has been found. The present church dates from the thirteenth century. At that time, like its Devonian namesake, Appledore was next to the sea. The draining and 'inning' (protecting with dykes or banks) of Romney Marsh caused the River Rother to change course and it was left high and dry for 500 years before the building of the Royal Military Canal in 1804.

Ashford's rise in recent years has been positively meteoric. A small market town from 1243 to the early nineteenth century, the building of the railway works in 1846, the arrival of the M20 and from 1996 the International rail station have turned it into a vital European centre.

Although its name has gone through a number of forms – in the Domesday survey it was Essetesford – it probably means what it looks like it means, a ford (on the Stour) where the ash trees were. It was important in ancient times to know where to walk off into a river, hence the identifying landmarks. On the other hand, the Stour was once known as the Eshe or Eshet, so you'd be wise not to take any chances.

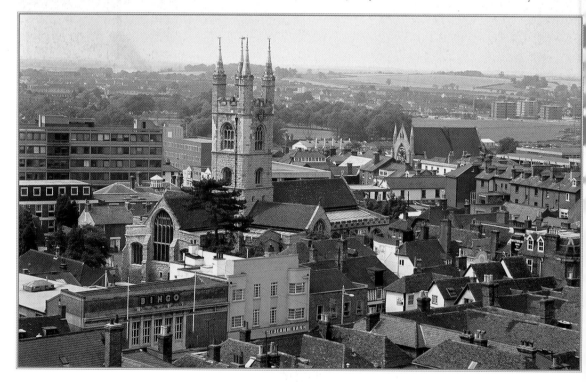

These pictures date from around 1970, when you could still weigh yourself in the street.
The church of St Mary the Virgin was restored in the fifteenth century.

Aylesford is a jewel of the Kent landscape and this view has been gracing cards and calendars for as long as there have been such things. Over the years it has become more and more like a stage set as, just off camera, paper-recycling works belch white smoke and traffic thunders along the M20 and the A229. In medieval times the ford was replaced with the only bridge (then) between Maidstone and Rochester, increasing both Aylesford's importance and the danger of attack from invaders. The original short tower of St Peter and St Paul's church was extended around then to improve its lookout potential.

Opposite: This photograph, taken at Beltring, shows some of the forty thousand hop-pickers who used to come to Kent every year, mainly from London. The huts with which they were provided were unfurnished, so they brought everything – children's toys, chairs, tables, even the family piano in some cases – on the back of a lorry or cart.

The Hop Farm at Beltring is the model of a modern 'heritage' tourist attraction. Its management works tirelessly to bring events and meetings to a location ideally suited to the purpose. Before it was a 'country park' it was a real, working hop farm. Whitbread owned it from the 1920s, but four of the five oasts date back to the nineteenth century – the fifth was added by them in 1936.

When I first saw Biddenden in the mid-1970s, I thought I'd arrived in paradise. If there is an ideal or typical English village, this could well be it. The Red Lion was built in 1415 by a veteran of the Battle of Agincourt. The singular village sign represents Eliza and Mary Chulkhurst, Britain's first recorded Siamese – or conjoined – twins. Daughters of a family of some substance, they became famous throughout the land and lived happily for thirty-odd years following their birth in around 1100.

Opposite: Brenchley is another gem of a village. Its name comes from Branca's Lea (meadow). Peasants' Revolt leader Wat Tyler is believed to have lived here in the fourteenth century. The combined butcher and greengrocery is a rare example of a long-surviving village shop.

As those of us who have read our *1066 And All That* know, invaders were forever coming ashore at Thanet. The Romans built forts there and the Vikings came so often they finally decided to stay and build such fishing ports as that which would become Bradstow – later Broadstairs. This is the 'Old Curiosity Shop' and the 'Wishing Well', which was the sole water supply in the old village. When the old cottages either side of it were incorporated, the well wound up indoors.

Broadstairs' other major industry was smuggling. Daniel Defoe noted that, of the 300 inhabitants, 27 were fishermen and the others had 'no visible means of support'. The present North Foreland lighthouse is a comparatively 'new' one, built in 1691 – the first was there in 1505.

Opposite: Still retaining much of the air of a perfect English seaside resort, before the arrival of the railways it was better known for shipbuilding. As the numbers of tourists dwindled, so the municipal brass band gave way to a bloke with a keyboard.

Not for nothing is the Archbishop of Canterbury the senior man (person) in the Church of England. Like much of Kent, this city was formed from soft and shifting ground, but doggedness and skill controlled the landscape and claimed it for one of Britain's most magnificent – certainly most significant – cathedrals.

Opposite: Canterbury Cathedral in the 1960s. The Roman advance party of 55BC found an already well-ordered and civilised Canterbury. As such, and because of its position, it had a particular importance to them when they returned for the full scale invasion in AD43. When the Romans left the Anglo-Saxons had no such sentimentality, and the place was abandoned for more than 100 years.

The cathedral in the early 1970s. Most of the buildings visible were there in the 1870s, though some have had the ends summarily carved off them. The town converted to Christianity in AD597, and the first cathedral was built as part of Christ Church Monastery in 602. It survived until around 1000, when it was destroyed by the Vikings. The first Danish king built a new one, which was lost in a fire the year after the Conquest. The cathedral that stands today was built by the Normans. Its first Archbishop was Thomas Becket.

A very 'sixties' image of the West Gate. Four years after Becket's death another fire struck the cathedral and no less a body than William of Sens was brought over to supervise the rebuilding. His choir was the first major Gothic building in England, though it was finished by his protégé, known as 'English William', following an accident that put the master out of action and led ultimately to his death.

The cathedral nowadays. The fabric stands unchanged. Now we can add theatrical lighting to the undiminished effects wrought on our senses by the medieval visionaries and craftsmen.

The priceless medieval glass was removed and put into storage in the Second World War, so when the cathedral was hit in an air raid in 1942 that blew in all the glass in the library, it was not the end of the world.

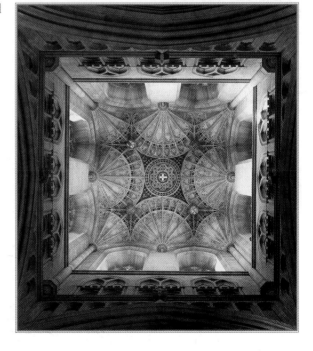

This photograph by the great John Edwards shows so clearly how fine the work of those old craftsmen was. Until the invention of precision optical equipment, few people would have been expected to see this work with such clarity. When they could – five hundred years after its completion – nothing was wanting. No short cuts had been taken.

St Augustine's Chair – the marble throne that is the seat of the Archbishop of Canterbury. The new archbishop was enthroned here on 27 February 2003.

The Norman staircase, an unusual survival of the dissolution, which once contained the water tower. The hall on the left was used by the cathedral's seneschal (cathedral official).

Difficult to believe when you see the gates of York, for example, but St George's Gate at Canterbury is the largest surviving city gate in England. There was an earlier one with a church on the top of it. This one dates from 1381. Even then, they had the foresight to make the arch big enough for a double-decker bus. This picture was taken in the 1960s with a Mini Countryman making the point.

The flint-built medieval Hospital of Thomas the Martyr (Eastbridge Hospital) is among the most beautiful buildings in a city with more than its share. With elements from the twelfth to the fourteenth centuries, it was constructed to provide quarters for poor pilgrims visiting the shrine and cathedral.

Another dimension of Canterbury can be discovered from the river with tours of the
ancient waterfronts such as the one leaving from Weaver's Bridge.

Opposite: This photograph was taken to commemorate the unveiling of the Canterbury
Festival Mural in 1984. It was painted just down from King's School Gate in King Street
by John Jones, with the assistance of Adam Taylor and senior students from the
Canterbury College of Art.

Above: At Charing, one tinder-dry hot summer's day in 1590, someone called Dios was trying to shoot a bird for the pot. He hit the church of St Peter and St Paul instead and started a fire so intense it melted the bells. The church was rebuilt and for nearly three hundred years had to make do with one bell. It now has six, given by Bishop Tufnell in 1878.

Archbishop Cranmer was forced to hand the Old Manor House over to Henry VIII. It had belonged to Canterbury since about 1330. Henry stayed there on the way to the 'Field of the Cloth of Gold' in 1520. The present owner of the house still extends the courtesy of allowing the archbishop to robe there when in Charing.

The village of Chiddingstone is now owned (since 1939) by the National Trust. Its High Street used to run in a straight line but was diverted in the late eighteenth century by Henry Streatfeild, then owner of the castle. A lake now exists where the street once stood.

The village of Chilham is a treasury of ancient buildings, often unnoticed by those passing on the A28. The Jacobean Castle was built for Sir Dudley Digges and has a curious hexagonal plan, with the sixth side acting as the entrance to the courtyard. Capability Brown designed the gardens and, in the eighteenth century, elephants were used to work the estate. The octagonal keep of the medieval castle is one of only two in England.

Pubs called the Woolpack abound in Kent. The one at Chilham dates from the fifteenth century and one of its fourteen bedrooms is said to be haunted by a 'Grey Lady'.

A 'Grey Gentleman' manifests himself from time to time at Chilham's other fifteenth-century inn, The White Horse. It sounds like a match made in limbo. He is believed to be the Rev. Sampson Hieron, whose vicarage the pub was until his death in 1677.

Chilham was the location and inspiration for Powell and Pressburger's 1944 feature film *A Canterbury Tale*, starring Eric Portman, Sheila Sim and Dennis Price.

Union Mill at Cranbrook got its name when its original owner, Henry Dobell, went bankrupt and the mill was taken over by a union of his creditors. The smock mill was built in 1814. At 75 feet tall, it is believed to have been the highest such mill in England.

Opposite: At the southern end of Sandwich Bay, Deal has guarded the east coast of Kent from Roman times. During the Napoleonic wars Nelson parleyed with Prime Minister Pitt at Walmer Castle, while Emma Hamilton awaited him at the Three Kings – now the Royal Hotel.

Dover Castle gazes down the centuries at the graceless buildings that had begun to afflict the town by the end of the '60s. The latest model has arrived at Austin House and the old ABC Cinema is still going in this picture from the early 1970s.

A White Cliffs experience. Fishing from Dover's Admiralty Pier.

Opposite: With the longest recorded history of any British fortress, the castle at Dover stands on a site first occupied in the iron age. As well as the Norman fortifications you see above ground, there is a network of tunnels in the supporting cliff, which were used in the Napoleonic wars and again in the Second World War.

Only one French car (Peugeot 403) on the quayside back then. That, too, would be somewhat different now. This shows two of Seaspeed's hovercraft being prepared for sea (or the air just above it). The inaugural crossings took place in July 1968. In 1981 Seaspeed, part of British Rail, absorbed its Ramsgate-based competitor, Hoverlloyd, to form Hoverspeed on Sunday 1 October 2000.

Below: Dover's Eastern Docks in the 1960s, long before the booze-cruise bonanza. Roll-on, roll-off freight had recently been introduced, dramatically streamlining cross-Channel cargo movement. A few hundred lorries passed through the port in 1965. In the early years of the twenty-first century the figure is closer to 1.8 million!

The old lighthouse at Dungeness viewed from the direction of the power station. A new lighthouse, the first to be built in the twentieth century, replaced it in 1960.

Like the sea it faces and the shingle to which it clings, Dungeness is in a continual state of flux. The balance of the community has changed over time and so have the buildings. Cottages that began life as single huts or railway carriages grow new wings and extensions that conceal their origins.

Opposite: The old foghorn has also now been replaced by an electronic affair. The effect, in a Dungeness fog, is no less eerie and has a certain extra-terrestrial quality.

Kentish seaside resorts have suffered more than most from the lure of the continent. Once people flocked to Dymchurch and it's still easy to see why. Its gentle sandy beach is ideal for families and it still has that English seaside atmosphere you won't find abroad.

Opposite: If you look above the shop fronts, Dymchurch has also got its share of venerable buildings. Like much of Romney Marsh, Dymchurch has a history of smuggling, and inspired the popular Dr Syn novels by Russell Thorndike.

The combination of the level crossing and the blind, single-track medieval bridge always makes driving through East Farleigh interesting. The Medway, now popular with boating types, runs through the very heart of hop country. The oasts here are mainly of the older, square variety. The stretch of river from here to Tonbridge also had a large concentration of fulling mills.

Opposite: Erith in the 1960s. American Hiram Maxim, a pioneer of powered flight who beat the Wright Brothers into the air (1898), became a naturalised British subject and was knighted in 1901. The inventor of the Maxim gun, he ran an armaments factory in Erith on the site of the present Europa Trading Estate.

Remains of the twelfth-century Lesnes Abbey at Erith.

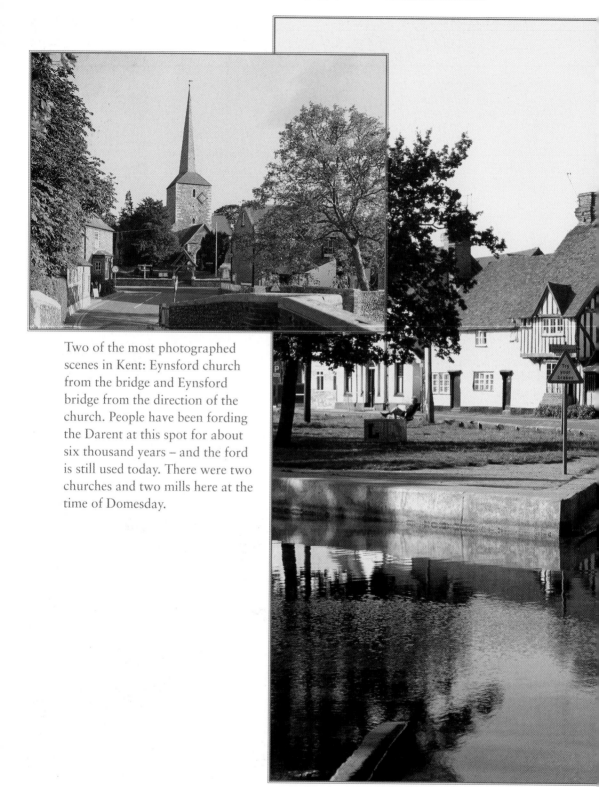

Two of the most photographed scenes in Kent: Eynsford church from the bridge and Eynsford bridge from the direction of the church. People have been fording the Darent at this spot for about six thousand years – and the ford is still used today. There were two churches and two mills here at the time of Domesday.

Conservation in action. Between these two pictures of Faversham's Guildhall being taken – the first in the 1960s, the second in the 1980s – the dome has been cleaned, the walls repainted and the TV aerials removed from nearby buildings. The earliest parts of the guildhall are Elizabethan, but there are elements from almost every century since, the last major remodelling having taken place in 1814.

The slender spire of St Mary of Charity church at Faversham was added in 1797 after
the original Early English nave had been declared unsafe. Modelled on Wren's
St Dunstan-in-the-East in London, it has the look of a Breton church from a distance.

More views of Faversham in the 1960s. One of the most successful amalgamations of
the ancient and the modern – especially now that traffic has been excluded from the
town centre – Faversham is now most famous as a beer town. England's oldest brewers,
Shepherd Neame, have been based here since 1698, and the annual hop festival is a
major event in the Kent calendar.

Until the railway arrived in Folkestone in 1843, it was a (predominantly mackerel)
fishing village, and this picture of the harbour in the early years of the twentieth century
records a time when that tradition lived on, side by side with tourism.

First built as The Leas Shelter in 1894, the Leas Cliff Hall had been expanded and refurbished to become a first class theatre and concert venue when this picture was taken in the 1920s.

Opposite: Folkestone built a reputation as one of the happiest of English seaside resorts. The elegance and sheer scale of its buildings and the variety of its landscape made it a fashionable resort, capable of catering to all. The monumental Grand and Metropole hotels here are among the finest such buildings in the land. Now that accommodation of this class on this scale is no longer needed, the Metropole provides the perfect location for an art gallery and a health centre.

The Zig-Zag, Folkestone's cliff walk in the 1920s. Always a popular promenade from
the top road to the bottom, going the other way was and is better done with the
Leas Lift.

Opposite: Folkestone old town is quite trendy now. This is what it looked like in about
1905. Even then it had become a curiosity to be visited from the new town.

In the old days it was possible to drive along the coast from Sandgate to Folkestone harbour by means of the toll road (Lower Sandgate Road). Nowadays it has been closed off and part of it turned into a car park that can only be reached from the harbour end.

The Old Town Hall at Fordwich – Britain's smallest town and, when Thanet was still an island, the port for Canterbury. On the right-hand end of this building, out of shot, is the crane that immersed and raised the Fordwich ducking stool.

Opposite: A forerunner of Debenham's, Bobbys on the corner of Sandgate Road in the 1930s. Parking on the wrong side of the road seems to have been the norm in those days. Now you dive into a cut-out bay if you get a chance, or keep going round the one-way system forever.

Two views of
Gillingham High
Street in the 1970s.
It is mostly
pedestrianised now
and traffic is
funnelled round on
the coastward side
toward Chatham
and the Medway
tunnel.

The pond at Goudhurst looking tranquil and somewhat overgrown before traffic levels reached their current nightmare proportions.

Goudhurst's Vine Hotel in the 1960s. It is rare to see this much of the A262 these days. The hotel dates mainly from the eighteenth century, though it incorporates older elements.

A view from further up the hill toward Goudhurst church and the sharp left-hander on the road to Ashford . . .

. . . and from the top looking back down toward the Vine Inn and the duck pond at the crossroads.

Loosely based on Big Ben, Gravesend's Clocktower was designed to commemorate Queen Victoria's golden jubilee. Its bells were donated by Alfred Tolhurst in 1890. Here it is in the '60s opposite Nottons dress shop, Pickford's removals and Burgess electricals, where you could buy an Ekco telly.

An historical gem among
the megastores and retail
parks, Gravesend's pier is
also now surrounded by
modern flats.

Hawkhurst before the First World War. Despite present traffic levels, it is hard to imagine this quiet country place as the home of the notorious six hundred-strong Hawkhurst Gang of smugglers in the eighteenth century. Two hundred years previously the likes of Sir Francis Drake visited here, staying at the Queens Hotel and playing on its bowling green, believed to be one of the oldest in England. The grass hump in the carriageway must have been a challenging obstacle on the unlit road.

An historic village on the main road from Maidstone to Tenterden, Headcorn suffered a terrible fire recently in one of the ancient half-timbered buildings in its High Street. Restoration and rebuilding complete, the horror of the skeletal black beams will soon fade from memory. The village church, dedicated to St Peter and St Paul, dates from the fifteenth century.

Opposite: Horsmonden in the late 1970s. Once a major centre of the Wealden ironworking industry, the village provided weapons for both sides in the English Civil War. Now slightly removed from the village, on the Goudhurst road, the church of St Margaret was built in the fourteenth century. The village centre moved with the building of the iron foundry in the sixteenth century.

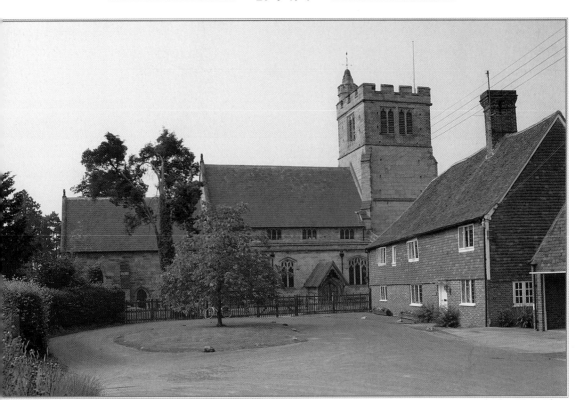

The Early English church of St Leonard presides over the ancient Cinque Port of Hythe in the early twentieth century. Over the centuries the church has expanded into the hillside, requiring more of what once was churchyard. This is a likely explanation for the presence in the crypt of stacks of human skulls.

In the 1950s traffic regulations were more discretionary. If you could get there, you could go there. Now the high street is semi-pedestrianised and one-way, and some of the side alleys are no longer passable, except on foot.

In the 1950s caravans were just that, rather than the centrally heated en suite gin palaces of today. And caravan sites were not surfaced and regimented as now. The entirely un-regimented Prince of Wales site seen here was named after the pub to which it was attached. Even in those less troubled times, it is not to be imagined that His Royal Highness stayed here.

Here's the pub, opposite Hythe Ranges, with the caravans in the field beyond.

Some distance from the main town, Hythe's seafront is still a model of elegance and resistance to commercialism.

The preserved Kent & East Sussex Railway opened in 1974 and runs from Tenterden to Bodiam, by way of Northiam. Here, across the bridge from Newenden, is also held the annual steam fair. At 11 miles, it is one of the longest preserved railways in Britain and there are plans to extend it to Robertsbridge.

With a long history stretching back to ancient drovers and swineherds who used this place as the crossing point of the River Teise, Lamberhurst is now building a new history for itself as a producer of English wines.

One of the most spectacular and beautiful fortified buildings in England, Leeds Castle
can now be seen from the M20. Built 900 years ago by a Norman baron, the castle was
a royal residence for three centuries. Moorish influences in its architecture are attributed
to Eleanor of Castile, wife of Edward I.

Littlebourne lies off the road from Canterbury to Sandwich. It is notable for the preservation of this fine eighteenth-century mill and Littlebourne Oast, both of which are unsurprisingly popular painting subjects.

Now requiring a slight detour off the A229 south of Maidstone, Loose is a secret paradise. Nestling in an unspoilt valley, it is a unique place of watercourses and walkways, wildfowl and wild flowers.

Maidstone gets its name from the Medway river. In Saxon times this was called
Medwege (middle river), hence Medwegeston (the enclosure or settlement upon it).

The Archbishops' Palace was built about the middle of the fourteenth century as a
residence for the Archbishops of Canterbury. All Saints' church which adjoins it dates
from the fifteenth century.

Castle Gate at Maidstone in the 1960s. More and more of Maidstone has been given over to car parking since this time.

Maidstone's tourist information centre is an attraction in itself, based as it is in the old gatehouse in Palace Gardens.

Maidstone's museum is named after Julius Brenchley, the nineteenth-century 'Gentleman Explorer' who donated the majority of its artefacts.

Mote Park is now a superbly landscaped public area, formerly the grounds of a house belonging to the Earl of Romney.

Opposite: Now rarely glimpsed through the nose-to-tail traffic, the Carriage Museum was donated to the town by Sir Garrard Tyrwhitt-Drake, an ex-Mayor of Maidstone. The first of its kind when it opened in 1946, it is housed in the stables of the Bishops' Palace – now cut off from it by the road.

St Michael and All Angels' parish church at Marden was built by the monks of Lesnes Abbey at Erith at the very end of the thirteenth century, using stone from the quarries at Boughton Monchelsea.

Opposite: Two views of Marden in the 1960s. Known as Meredenne at the time of the Conquest, it was in the hands of the Crown until James I's time. The Unicorn Inn dates from the seventeenth century.

The fish and chips image of Margate disseminated by the likes of Chas and Dave diverts attention from the history and architectural interest of this north coast town.

Like that in Gravesend, the clock tower on
Margate seafront was built to commemorate
Queen Victoria's jubilee.

THE OLD TOWN BOOKSHOP

An unmissable feature of the Darent Valley between Farningham and Sevenoaks, everyone knows Otford for its village duckpond with built-in detached accommodation, but there are also remains of another old palace of the Archbishops of Canterbury, rebuilt in 1501.

The parish church of St John the Baptist at Penshurst was built in 1120, almost certainly on the site of an earlier one. The bell tower contains a stone coffin lid known as 'the smiling lady of Penshurst'. This is thought to be connected with the Albigensians – also known as Cathars – from Albi in France, and dates from the thirteenth century.

With the fourteenth-century Penshurst Place at its heart, Penshurst has managed to survive the centuries with much of its spirit intact. Kent tile and oak beams, leaded lights and ragstone provide setting and support for the towering hollyhocks.

This image of the parish church of St Margaret at Rainham makes it look somewhat
overgrown and bucolic. Behind us, unsuspected, is the hubbub and mayhem of the A2.
Things were not always thus, of course, in the 700 years since the church was built.

St Augustine's in Ramsgate is considered to be the masterpiece of Victorian architect Augustus Welby Pugin.

St Augustine came ashore at Ebbsfleet in the sixth century. The event is celebrated in Ramsgate, not only by the church and the abbey, but also by the golf course named after him. Ramsgate's fortunes have been a bit up and down in recent years. Like other places on the east coast, tourism has waned, most holidaymakers coming this far being intent on crossing the Channel. The biggest blow came when Sally Line ceased its crossings to Dunkerque.

In 604 that same St Augustine established Rochester as England's second bishopric after Canterbury. The present cathedral is quite bijou by comparison to the likes of Canterbury, but contains elements of just about every architectural style from the eleventh century onwards.

Here's a conundrum: it is to be assumed that the picture here with the car in it is later, because of the double yellow lines. This would also make sense if the weather vane had been removed. But the building on the left looks as if it has had a nameboard put over the 'Limited' carved into its frontage, and the shield has been removed from above the door. Then again, the lamp post has been removed. . . . Either way, the Clock House and clock were given to Rochester in the eighteenth century by no less an historical body than Sir Cloudesley Shovel, the most respected admiral of his day.

College Ward, Rochester, in the 1960s. Despite its air of seriousness, Rochester is also a place of entertainment and celebration, as in the annual Sweeps and Dickens festivals.

Rolvenden post office in the 1970s. The Nat West has gone and the post office has combined with the Mace shop to form the village stores.

If it wasn't for the TV aerials, this 1960s picture of St Mary the Virgin at Rolvenden could be from much earlier in the last century. Built in the fourteenth century, the present church features an upstairs pew for the Lord of the Manor. Rolvenden was among the first villages to embrace the idea of farmers' markets, which took place in the church until the new village hall was competed.

St Clement's church at Old Romney is 800 years old and the yew tree is much the same age.

Coronation Square, Lydd, in the 1980s. Lydd was an island long before Romney Marsh was 'inned' and there is evidence for a Roman settlement here.

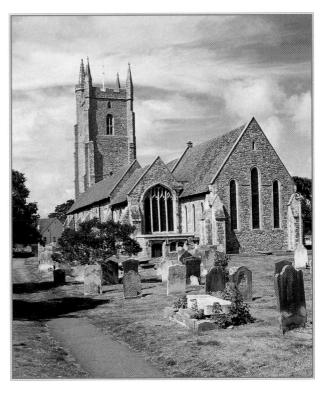

Lydd is the most southerly town in Kent and All Saints' church is the longest in the county. Famous as the 'Cathedral of the Marsh', it is not really on Romney Marsh. Lydd is built on the same shingle bank as Dungeness, with Walland Marsh to the north and Denge Marsh to the south. Romney Marsh proper lies to the east of the Rhie Wall (A259) and Old and New Romney.

Captain Howey and Count Zborowski were both racing drivers. In 1924 they made a pact that they would give it up and build a 15 inch gauge railway. With the aid of Henry Greenly, who designed the railway, they achieved their goal.

In July 1927 the first train ran on the Romney, Hythe and Dymchurch Railway. A year or so later the line was extended to Dungeness.

The twin towers of the old monastic church at Reculver have long been a landmark for sailors, although its ecclesiastical uses ended in the nineteenth century.

St Margaret's Bay
in the 1960s. Quiet
then, and still so
today, it is a perfect
place to come and
stare at the sea. In
times gone by it
was more active,
when smugglers
descended from
St Margaret's-at-
Cliffe. The white
cliffs – just around
the corner from
Dover – contain
caves ideal for the
concealment of
contraband.

The idea for a Channel tunnel is not new. There have been various schemes in the past
and one of them would have involved Sandgate. Rather than come up on shore, however,
the English end was planned to arrive on a man-made island with a drawbridge
connecting it to the mainland. That way, if we fell out with the French – which was very
nearly all we did with them for many centuries – we could raise a drawbridge and prevent
them coming ashore. Actually they would have fitted in nicely with the preference of
Sandgate drivers in the 1960s for parking on the right – even next to the 'keep left' sign.

Looking in the opposite direction, toward Hythe, it's interesting to note the importance
of the coal order office and the Esso sign along the street.

Present before the arrival of the Romans, until the River Stour silted up Sandwich was one of the most important ports in England. The Barbican guards the bridge into the town.

The King's Arms in Sandwich started out in 1592 as the Queen's Arms, so named for Queen Elizabeth I who visited this part of the town. It cannot be inferred from the name change that there was any truth in the rumours about Her Majesty.

This is Sandwich in the 1950s, with a Commer – or possibly a Leyland Comet – belonging to the then nationalised South Eastern Gas Board parked on the quayside.

The Old House at Sandwich is recognised as a model of Tudor design. This picture is from the early twentieth century.

The Quay at Sandwich in the early twentieth century. It was from here that English
monarchs and their armies took ship for France in the days when monarchs
accompanied their armies.

This view of Scotney Castle is known the world over. Construction of the castle was begun by Roger Ashburnham in around 1380.

Opposite: Sevenoaks in around 1904, when its streets were more than adequate for the volume of traffic. Priorities were different then as evidenced by the two dairies, one each side of London Road. Lloyd's Bank had a serious presence on the High Street, too.

By the 1960s Victoria Wine and Russell & Bromley were firmly established in Sevenoaks.

The Kingsferry Bridge to Sheppey over Long Reach when it was still relatively new.
Opened in 1960 and originally owned by British Rail, it is one of only two such bridges
in the world with a vertically lifting mid-section.

Can this be another jubilee clock tower? No, in short. The one in Sheerness was built to commemorate the coronation of King Edward VII in 1902 and is the largest free standing clock of its type in Kent.

The bridge over the Darent at Shoreham. In 1827 the artist Samuel Palmer, suffering from ill-health, moved to what he called his 'valley of vision' and began his most productive period.

The gardens at Sissinghurst were created by Vita Sackville-West and Harold Nicolson in the 1930s. The name means 'clearing in the woods' and the house was built in the fifteenth century. The nearby Bull Inn was made famous by Jeffrey Farnol in his novel *The Broad Highway*. Its publication in 1910 caused Farnol, who had been working as a scene painter in America for eight years, to return to England – and write another thirty-five novels!

A lone airman sits on the boss of a gigantic aeroplane propeller at Capel-le-Ferne and
gazes at the skies above Folkestone where the Battle of Britain was fought in 1940.
It took over half a century for this memorial to the last major conflict on British soil to
be put in place. It was unveiled by HRH The Queen Mother in 1993.

Opposite: Like Appledore, Smallhythe was once a seaport, renowned for its
shipbuilding. When the Rother changed its course Smallhythe was up the creek.
Smallhythe Place was once the Customs House. In 1899 it was bought by the
actress Dame Ellen Terry, who lived there until her death in 1929. It is now a museum
to her.

The George & Dragon at Speldhurst is claimed to be the second oldest inn in England (after the Fountain at Canterbury). Dating originally from 1212, it started out as a Wealden hall house. Standing opposite Speldhurst church, with its windows by Burne-Jones, it was known simply as the Old Inn before receiving its present name in 1800. The York stone flags in its downstairs bar came from the old London Bridge.

The Fuller House and Maplehurst are among the superb half-timbered houses that surround the thirteenth-century church at Staplehurst.

Tenterden in the late 1960s. Now far removed from the sea, the town once enjoyed Cinque Port privileges. Its quay was at Smallhythe. The wide main street must be one of the most gracious in England. The Town Hall building (with the balcony) dates from 1790; the church, dedicated to St Mildred, the second abbess of Minster, was built in the fifteenth century and has a 100 foot tower.

The ancient seven-arched bridge at Teston, between Tonbridge and Maidstone on the Medway. Next to it now is a car park and riverside walk.

A timeless landmark, visible from large areas of Thanet, Sarre Windmill, built in 1820, is fully restored and still earns a living grinding corn.

Even timeless things don't stay the same. Tonbridge Castle was built soon after the Norman Conquest – and rebuilt following a fire twenty-odd years later. Its keep has decayed gradually over the centuries, but the most noticeable difference between this picture, taken in the 1930s . . .

. . . and this one from the 1980s is the jagged outline exposed by the removal of the softening greenery. The fashion for nakedness in old buildings is very much of our time, and can be useful in dating such images.

St Peter's church at Tonbridge in the 1930s and again in the 1960s. The stone church
was built in 1124 on the site of an earlier Saxon structure.

The Tudor Chequers Inn in the 1930s was tied to Maidstone brewers Style & Winch. Electric milk floats, such as this one belonging to Tonbridge Dairy, were the latest thing and remained in use at least until the 1950s. The milkman walked in front.

By the 1960s Aplin's Tudor Café had become Cobleys and the Chequers had hijacked the Style & Winch 'gallows' for their own shield.

Interesting to note in this image of the footpath between the castle and the river, there is a 'Gunners' shop, further up the road and on the opposite side to the one in the older picture of the Chequers.

Originally founded in 1553 by Sir Andrew Judde, Tonbridge School occupies about
150 acres to the north of Tonbridge. The majority of its buildings date from the late
nineteenth century. When this picture was taken the new Smythe Library had recently
been completed (1962).

Wisely pedestrianised early on, The Pantiles in Tunbridge Wells gets its name from the
square tiles with which it was originally surfaced. They were replaced with the present
flagstones in 1793. Here is the entrance to the wells from which the town gets its name.

The other most notable feature of Tunbridge Wells is the quantity of open space and parkland with which it is surrounded. These pictures of Mount Ephraim in the 1960s recall a time when it was not also surrounded by cars.

This was photographed in about 1970. Do you think the signwriter meant to say 'Peking Restaurant'?

One of the extraordinary overhanging rocks on the Common at Tunbridge Wells.

Sir Winston Churchill lived at Chartwell near Westerham. When this bronze statue of him by Oscar Nemon was unveiled in 1969, virtually the entire population of Westerham turned out to see it.

General Wolfe, who won Canada for the British by defeating the French in Quebec, was born at Westerham Vicarage.

St Mary the Virgin, Westerham, parts of which date from the thirteenth century, contains a memorial window to Wolfe, designed by Burne-Jones.

Opposite: The Old Town Hall and St Mildred's Bay, Westgate-on-Sea, in the 1960s. Named after the abbess of Minster, the bay is also famous for St Mildred's Baths – a 70-foot-long swimming pool containing 60,000 gallons of tepid seawater.

These two hauntingly atmospheric pictures were taken on the same day at Whitstable Harbour. The time is probably the 1920s. What looks like a traveller's wagon on the quayside is actually a covered railway truck and there are also two steamboats visible.

Millers Court on Borstal Hill, Whitstable, in the 1960s. Note the patterned shutters, still a feature of old buildings in parts of Europe. The mill has long offered accommodation and it is believed that Douglas Fairbanks Senior stayed here on his honeymoon. It is still a B&B to this day, though it has lost the flat-roofed extension and – somewhat bizarrely – gained a tail-wheel.

The King's Head at Wye in the 1960s. The church was rebuilt and enlarged in the thirteenth century. When Archbishop Kemp built Wye College in 1447 he added matching windows to the church.

Kemp's college was a residence for priests. It now houses the agricultural department of London University.

Opposite: Two views of Yalding, another gem of the Kent countryside, unfortunately better known for the devastating floods that have afflicted it in recent years than for its intrinsic beauty. The main contribution of modern times to these pictures is the gross – and largely unnecessary – painting of double yellow lines all over the village's ancient bridges.